ANNE FRANK

By Jonatha A. Brown

WORLD ALMANAC® LIBRARY

Please visit our web site at: www.worldalmanaclibrary.com
For a free color catalog describing World Almanac® Library's list
of high-quality books and multimedia programs, call 1-800-848-2928 (USA)
or 1-800-387-3178 (Canada). World Almanac® Library's fax: (414) 332-3567.

Library of Congress Cataloging-in-Publication Data

Brown, Jonatha A.
  Anne Frank / by Jonatha A. Brown.
    p. cm. — (Trailblazers of the modern world)
  Includes bibliographical references and index.
  Summary: A biography of Anne Frank, including the historical events which forced her to hide
with her family in an attic in Nazi-occupied Holland for two years.
    ISBN 0-8368-5090-4 (lib. bdg.)
    ISBN 0-8368-5250-8 (softcover)
    1. Frank, Anne, 1929-1945—Juvenile literature. 2. Jewish children in the Holocaust—Netherlands—
Amsterdam—Biography—Juvenile literature. 3. Jews—Netherlands—Amsterdam—Biography—Juvenile
literature. 4. Jewish girls—Netherlands—Amsterdam—Biography—Juvenile literature. 5. Amsterdam
(Netherlands)—Biography—Juvenile literature. [1. Frank, Anne, 1929-1945. 2. Jews—Netherlands—
Biography. 3. Holocaust, Jewish (1939-1945)—Netherlands—Amsterdam. 4. Women—Biography.]
  I. Title. II. Series.
  DS135.N6F7323   2003
  940.53'18'092—dc21
  [B]   2003041184

First published in 2004 by
World Almanac® Library
330 West Olive Street, Suite 100
Milwaukee, WI 53212 USA

Copyright © 2004 by World Almanac® Library.

Project manager: Jonny Brown
Editor: Jim Mezzanotte
Design and page production: Scott M. Krall
Photo research: Diane Laska-Swanke
Indexer: Walter Kronenberg

Photo credits: © Anne Frank Fonds-Basel/Anne Frank House-Amsterdam/Getty Images: cover, 5, 8 bottom, 9 both,
13, 14, 19 both, 20, 22 both, 23, 24 all, 25 both, 26, 28; © Bettmann/CORBIS: 12 top, 35; © Hulton Archive/Getty
Images: 4, 8 top, 11, 12 bottom, 15, 16, 18, 21, 31, 33, 34, 36, 37, 38, 39, 43; © Hulton-Deutsch Collection/CORBIS:
10; Photographic assistance: Anthony E. Anderson: 17, 30; © Andy Rain/Getty Images: 42

Printed in the United States of America

1 2 3 4 5 6 7 8 9 07 06 05 04 03

TABLE of CONTENTS

Words that appear in the glossary are printed in **boldface** type the first time they occur in the text.

CHAPTER 1

LIVING WITH FEAR

Foreign troops have taken control of your country. They soon begin identifying all Jewish people, which includes you, your family, and many others in your community. What will the future bring?

A LIFE IN PERIL

The invaders make life increasingly difficult for Jews. They force your father to sign over his business to a non-Jewish person. They pass laws meant only for Jews. You are forbidden to ride a bicycle or shop at your favorite stores, and you can be arrested if you go outside after 8:00 at night. As the situation worsens, soldiers begin knocking on doors, taking ordinary adults and children out of their homes, and sending them to what they call "work camps." Many of those who are taken away will never return.

You are very frightened, and so are your parents. They must protect you and themselves, but how can they? They are not allowed to leave the country, they have no weapons with which to fight, and they have been cut off from their friends. No escape seems possible.

Your parents are desperate. Early one morning they wake you up, tell you to put on as many layers of clothing as you can, and lead you away. As you walk through your city, they explain that you will not be going home again for many months, perhaps years.

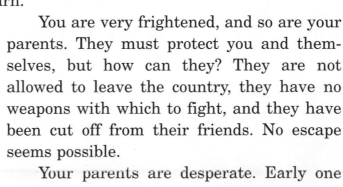

When German soldiers arrived in May 1940, frightened residents of this Dutch town stayed inside their houses.

Your mind is full of questions. Where are you going? What will happen to you? And what about the kitten you left behind? Will he starve? You beg your parents to go back for the cat, but they cannot. If you return home again, you might be arrested, even shot. You must get to a safe and secret place as quickly as possible.

You reach your hideout at last. Here it is—a few tiny, unused rooms above the offices and warehouse of what was once your father's business. These rooms are now your sanctuary. As long as the enemy does not know you are here, you are safe. But these cramped little rooms are also your prison. You cannot go outside or even look out a window. You cannot make the slightest noise when workers might be around. You most certainly cannot contact your friends.

Weeks and months pass. The enemy still controls your country, and you remain in hiding. It is a nearly unbearable existence, both terrifying and boring, but for now, at least, you are alive. Hundreds of thousands of others who could not hide have already died.

A LIFE CUT SHORT

Such a way of life might be hard to imagine, but it was once a terrifying reality for thousands of people. Little more than fifty years ago, when World War II (1939–1945) was raging, many Jewish children in various parts of Europe lived in hiding as they tried to escape certain death at the hands of the German **Nazis**. Anne Frank was one of those children.

When this photograph was taken, in October 1942, Anne Frank was thirteen years old and dreamed of being a movie star. Next to the picture she wrote, "This is a photo as I wish myself to look all the time. Then I would have a chance to come to Hollywood."

Dit is een foto, zoals
ik me zou wensen,
altijd zo te zijn.
Dan had ik nog wel
een kans om naar
Hollywood te komen.

Anne Frank.
10 Oct. 1942

(translation)
"This is a photo as I would wish
self to look all the time. Then
would maybe have a chance to
 to Hollywood."
Anne Frank, 10 Oct. 1942

Anne was a Jewish girl whose family had moved to the Netherlands in the 1930s. The Germans invaded this country in 1940 and soon began to **persecute** the Netherlands' Jews. When the situation became too threatening, the Franks tried to escape by going into hiding. With the help of non-Jewish friends, they stayed out of sight for over two years. Finally, however, they were betrayed, and the Nazis sent the whole family to **concentration camps**. Anne died in one of those camps a few months later. She was fifteen years old.

A LIFE RECORDED

When the Franks were arrested and taken from their hideout, they inadvertently left something important behind: Anne's diary. This diary was a record of Anne's life during the twenty-five months she spent hiding from the Nazis. After her arrest, friends found the diary and saved it. Later, it was published in many languages, and readers all over the world were deeply touched by the story of Anne, her family, and several friends as they struggled for survival. Anne's story was also adapted for the stage and film, allowing it to reach an even wider audience. The book, as well as the play and movie based on it, helped people understand the enormity of the **Holocaust** and the Nazis' crimes against millions of innocent men, women, and children.

After reading the diary or seeing the play or movie, people everywhere felt a sense of personal loss. For them, Anne Frank's story gave a face, a voice, and a personality to at least one Holocaust victim. Although the Nazis murdered thousands of well-known and accomplished adults, it was Anne Frank—a previously anonymous teenaged girl—who eventually became one of the most famous victims of Nazi atrocities.

EARLY LIFE IN GERMANY

Anne's father, Otto, grew up in Frankfurt, Germany, where his ancestors had lived for generations. When Otto was young, his Jewish family was upper middle class, almost rich. They owned a bank, managed a few small businesses, and lived in a large, elegant house. During World War I (1914–1918), both Otto and his brother were proud to serve in the German army and buy bonds that helped finance the war.

Otto Frank married Edith Hollander in 1925. She came from Aachen, Germany, where her father was a respected leader of the city's Jewish community.

GERMANY'S ECONOMIC SITUATION

After the Germans lost World War I, the victors—including England, France, and Italy—forced Germany to give up much valuable territory and most of its foreign investments. They also forced Germany to pay them billions of dollars for war damages. To pay this debt, Germany printed more and more paper money, but the new money was nearly worthless. Costs within Germany rose, people such as the Franks saw their wealth shrink, and unemployment became a serious issue. Many German citizens were unhappy, and some took part in uprisings against the government.

The Rising Cost of a Loaf of Bread

In 1918, a loaf of bread in Germany cost about half a mark (a unit of German money). By 1922, the price was 163 marks per loaf. By November 1923, a loaf of bread in Germany cost millions of marks. With this drastic **inflation**, some Germans could only afford to eat cabbage, and many could not afford fuel for cooking and heating. They were hungry, cold, and discouraged.

Like other German businesses, the Franks' bank suffered serious losses after the war. By the time Otto and Edith married, however, the situation was improving. The newlyweds were soon able to afford a place of their own. They moved from Otto's mother's house to a spacious apartment, and they hired a live-in housekeeper.

After World War I, many Germans could not afford skyrocketing costs, such as rents. This German family had to live in a stable next to livestock.

Otto and Edith Frank with baby Margot in 1926

FAMILY LIFE

The housekeeper's help was important, since Otto and Edith's family was growing. Their first daughter, Margot Betti, was born in 1926. Three years later, on June 12, 1929, another baby girl—Annelies (Anne) Marie—made the family complete. The two little girls were the center of Otto and Edith's lives.

Unlike most men of his time, Otto was a very active and devoted father. When the babies cried late at night, Otto often took care of them. He loved playing games with his daughters, as well as inventing stories to entertain them and taking pictures to put in the family album. In Anne's opinion, he was "the most adorable father I've ever seen."

Margot and Anne had very different personalities. Whereas Margot was easygoing, cheerful, and quiet, Anne could be stubborn and demanding. She was easily bored and distracted, full of energy, and a non-stop talker. Her parents called Anne

"a mass of contradictions"—impishly charming when she was happy and annoyingly whiny when she was not. As she grew older, it became clear that she was also very opinionated. As a neighbor used to say, "God knows everything, but Anne knows everything better."

The two girls had plenty of playmates. Jews made up only about 6 percent of Frankfurt's population, however, so Margot and Anne mostly played with Catholic and Protestant children. The Frank girls sometimes participated in their friends' Christian celebrations, and their friends came to the Franks' home for **Hanukkah** festivities.

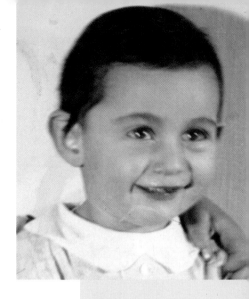

Anne as a toddler in 1931

THE GREAT DEPRESSION

Like most young children, Margot and Anne did not really understand what was happening in the world around them. They did not realize, for example, that a few months after Anne's birth, a worldwide economic crisis called the **Great Depression** had begun. The girls also did not know that, by 1932 (when Anne was three years old), industrial production in Germany had fallen by 65 percent and millions of Germans had lost their jobs. The economic situation had become worse than it had been right after World War I.

The Franks' bank lost over 90 percent of its business during this depression.

Margot and Anne Frank in 1933

With less money coming in, Otto had to move the bank to a smaller space and move his family to a smaller apartment. An increasing number of Germans, however, were suffering far more than the Franks. Extremely poor, unable to find steady work, and still humiliated by the loss of World War I, they began to lose confidence in the German government.

HITLER'S RISE TO POWER

During the postwar years, a **prejudiced** and persuasive man named Adolf Hitler gained attention. Although born and raised in Austria, Hitler had become a fiercely patriotic German. He believed Germany was the best

Adolf Hitler, the *Führer*, or absolute ruler, of Nazi Germany

nation on Earth and that ethnically "pure" Germans—blond-haired, blue-eyed people of Northern European descent, whom he called Aryans—were the strongest, smartest race in the world. Hitler despised most other ethnic groups, especially Jewish people. He once wrote that he "hated the motley collection of Czechs, Ruthenians, Poles, Hungarians, Serbs, Croats, and above all that ever-present fungoid growth—Jews."

By 1921, Hitler was leading the National Socialist German Workers' Party, whose members were called Nazis. He made fiery political speeches in which he blamed the Jews for Germany's defeat in World War I as well as for the country's postwar economic problems. He also criticized Germany's leaders and claimed that only the Nazis could bring prosperity to the struggling nation.

At first, most German citizens paid little attention to Hitler's wild accusations and promises. Later, however, as the country continued to flounder, more and more people took his ideas seriously, and his popularity rose. In the 1932 elections to the Reichstag (Germany's **parliament**), the Nazi Party won more votes than any other political party. Shortly after this victory, Hitler was appointed chancellor, or leader, of Germany.

Persecution of Jews

For centuries, Jews have been the targets of religious persecution, especially from people of the Christian faith. Many Christians have been suspicious of Jews because Jews refuse to convert to Christianity and are, therefore, "different." In some societies, Jews have become scapegoats, falsely accused of being the cause of all kinds of problems. Jews have been called "Christ killers" and have even been accused of absurd, horrible crimes, such as sucking children's blood or killing children for use in rituals. When **anti-Semitism** has been especially strong, Jews have become targets of large-scale, organized campaigns of persecution, such as the **pogroms** of Russia. In many of these instances, Jewish people have been isolated, humiliated, and even murdered.

Although Hitler's persecution of Jews was not a new idea, it was different in one important way. Unlike many before him, Hitler did not preach hatred of the Jews because of their religious faith. Instead, he insisted they were an inferior race of people and that their inherited traits, not their religion, made them Jews. According to Hitler, if even one of your grandparents was Jewish, then your blood was tainted—you were a Jew.

This fourteenth-century drawing depicts Jews killing Christian children in order to use their blood for ghastly ceremonies. At the time, many Christians believed such events actually happened.

CHAPTER 3

EMIGRATION TO THE NETHERLANDS

In 1933, the Nazi-dominated Reichstag passed a law that allowed Hitler to ignore Germany's democratic constitution and take control of the government. Once the law was passed, changes came quickly. Hitler suspended the right of people to gather and speak freely. He also formed the Gestapo, a police force that used terror tactics to control the German people.

Followers of Hitler (center) greet him with the Nazi salute in 1933 Berlin.

In 1933, soldiers and civilians in Germany burn a huge pile of "non-Aryan" books banned by the Nazis. Many of the books were written by Jews.

He outlawed all political parties other than the Nazi Party and sent the Gestapo after his political enemies. Soon, thousands were being arrested, beaten, and imprisoned in concentration camps. Hitler had become a powerful **dictator**. His control over ordinary citizens' lives was virtually complete.

One of Hitler's goals was to make Germany *Judenrein*—"free of Jews." As a first step, the Nazis declared a one-day boycott of Jewish businesses. Then the Nazis barred Jews from teaching or working in government jobs. They banned books by Jewish writers and used book burnings to generate public hostility against the writings of Jews and other "enemies" of the state. The Nazis also printed strongly anti-Semitic articles in newspapers, and they spoke against Jews both in public addresses and in radio broadcasts. During the early 1930s, the purpose of the

Nazis' campaign was simple—to harass and frighten Jews into leaving Germany. Soon, however, fleeing all of Europe would become the only way that Jews and other minorities could find true safety.

The Nazi Propaganda Machine

In order for Hitler and his fellow Nazis to successfully control Germany, they had to get as many German citizens as possible to accept their views. To win over the citizenry, the Nazis used **propaganda** to prey on the German people's traditional fears, suspicions, and prejudices involving Jews and other ethnic minorities.

The Nazis took over German newspapers and controlled every article the papers printed. They also took over the film, radio, arts, book publishing, and tourism industries. By controlling these industries, the Nazis could shape the information the German people received and deliver only one kind of message—the kind that supported their cause.

LEAVING THE COUNTRY

Edith Frank with Anne (left) and Margot, in Germany, 1933

By early 1933, Otto and Edith Frank no longer felt safe in Germany. When Otto learned of a business opportunity in the Netherlands—a country west of Germany whose citizens were generally tolerant of Jews—he and Edith decided to move there. Later that year, Otto went to the Netherlands' capital city, Amsterdam. He started a new business, found an apartment, and then sent for Edith, Margot, and Anne.

Writing about the experience in her diary a few years later, Anne explained that her parents went to the Netherlands "in September, while Margot and I were sent to Aachen [Germany] to stay with our grandmother. Margot went to Holland [the Netherlands] in December, and I followed in February, when I was plunked down on the table as a birthday present for Margot." After only a few months apart, the family was together again.

LIVING IN THE NETHERLANDS

The Frank girls were seven and four years old when they moved to Amsterdam. Being somewhat shy, Margot had more trouble settling into her new home. "Anne has made the adjustment better than Margot," their mother wrote to friends. Soon, however, both children learned to speak Dutch (the language of the Netherlands) and began attending school. In a letter written in 1935, Edith reported that "Anne is learning to read with great difficulty." Even so, Anne liked school and did well in most subjects. She and Margot had many friends.

Anne in Amsterdam in 1935, smiling for the camera as she plays with a Dutch friend

Anne, unfortunately, was a frail child. Year after year, illnesses such as chicken pox, measles, flu, and fevers kept her out of school for days at a time. One of her girlfriends, Hanneli Goslar (called Lies for short), often visited when Anne was sick at home. Lies brought Anne's homework assignments and shared the latest news about their friends. Years later, Lies remembered that during those visits, Anne "was always very cheerful. She loved little secrets and she loved to chat."

While Anne and Margot were experiencing the ordinary ups and downs of childhood, their parents were struggling. Edith had trouble learning Dutch and was often homesick, and Otto had to be away from home more than he liked. His new business, Opekta, sold pectin to housewives, who used it to make homemade jams and jellies. Sales were often slow. Otto could not afford to hire salesmen, so he traveled around the Netherlands alone to sell his product.

Despite these difficulties, life for the family-oriented Franks was good. They vacationed at the seashore and took a houseboat tour on the Dutch canals. Otto taught Margot and Anne funny songs, and he played with them and helped them when they needed advice or comfort. Edith, meanwhile, attended **synagogue** regularly, usually with Margot. Both Anne and her father were not interested in attending religious services, so they usually stayed home.

This photograph shows the smashed windows of a Jewish shop in Berlin. It was taken after *Kristallnacht*, a night of widespread, anti-Jewish rioting on November 9, 1938.

Persecution of Jews in Nazi Germany

The Nazis took many harsh measures against Jews in Germany. In 1933, they organized a boycott of Jewish businesses and made it illegal for Jews to teach or to work for the government. In 1935, the Nazis passed laws that revoked German citizenship for Jews and forbade marriage between Jews and non-Jews. In November 1938, the Nazis stirred mobs of Germans into a frenzy that resulted in *Kristallnacht* ("the Night of Broken Glass")—a night of widespread riots in which thousands of Jewish shops and synagogues were robbed and burned. By the end of 1938, Jewish children were no longer allowed to attend schools with Christian children.

In Germany, the Nazis were growing stronger, and Jews were suffering under a growing number of repressive laws. Thousands of Jews fled to other countries between 1933 and 1937, but as the years went by, Jews in Germany had difficulty finding safe havens. Most nations did not want too many **refugees**, so they stopped accepting Jewish immigrants. With nowhere to go, German Jews were essentially trapped.

Hitler, meanwhile, was building a strong army and expanding his empire. Between 1936 and 1939, German troops took over the Rhineland (a territory Germany had lost in World War I), Austria, and Czechoslovakia. Finally, after Hitler's army entered Poland on September 1, 1939, Britain and France declared war on Germany. World War II had begun.

During the early years of the war, Hitler's forces swiftly conquered many countries. In the spring of 1940, German troops invaded Denmark, Norway, the Netherlands, Belgium, and France. The Netherlands—a country that had seemed so safe to the Franks—fell to the Germans after just five days of fighting.

German soldiers in the Dutch city of Rotterdam in 1940

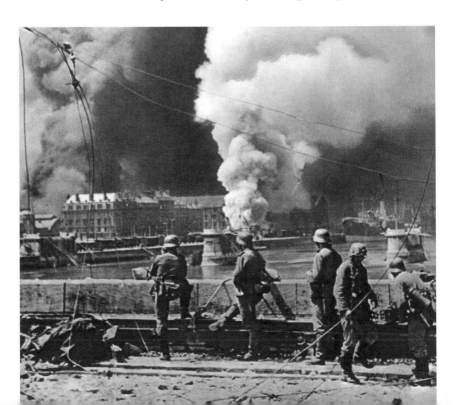

PERSECUTION

When the Germans invaded the Netherlands, the Dutch were stunned and frightened. They did not know what to expect, but they did not think a German occupation would be pleasant. Soon, however, they noticed that the soldiers who patrolled their streets were not harassing them. Then they heard the German governor of the Netherlands publicly declare, "We Germans have not come to subjugate this country and its people, nor do we seek to impose our political system on them." Hoping for the best, most Dutch citizens returned to their everyday lives and waited for Great Britain and other free countries to rescue them.

CHANGES FOR THE NETHERLANDS' JEWS

In January 1941, life began to change for Jews in the Netherlands when the Nazis issued a simple but sinister order: all Jews (including anyone with at least one Jewish grandparent) had to register with the new government. Accustomed to obeying the law and afraid to do otherwise, almost all Jews reported their names and addresses to the Nazis. When this registration was complete, the Nazi predators knew exactly where to find their Jewish prey.

During the Nazi occupation of the Netherlands, every person had to have an identification card. The letter "J" in the top right and bottom left corners of this card clearly identifies the cardholder as a Jew.

Armed with names and addresses, the Nazis began to harass Dutch Jews. They forced Jews out of their jobs and made them sell their businesses. They took control of Jewish bank accounts, forbade Jews from associating with Aryans, and barred them from more and more public places. Thousands of Jews lost their jobs, their savings, their property, and their non-Jewish friends.

Anne Describes the Restrictions

On June 15, 1942, Anne listed some of the ways the Nazis were restricting the activities of Dutch Jews. "After May 1940," she wrote, "the good times were few and far between: Jews were required to wear a yellow star [and] turn in their bicycles; Jews were forbidden to use streetcars [and] ride in cars, even their own; Jews were required to do their shopping between 3 and 5 p.m. [and] frequent only Jewish-owned barbershops and beauty parlors; Jews were forbidden to be out on the streets between 8 p.m. and 6 a.m.; . . . to attend theaters, movies or any other forms of entertainment, . . . to use swimming pools . . . [or] take part in any athletic activity in public; Jews were forbidden to sit in their gardens or those of their friends after 8 p.m.; . . . [and they] were required to attend Jewish schools, etc. . . . . [My friend] Jacque always said to me, 'I don't dare do anything anymore, 'cause I'm afraid it's not allowed.'"

Wearing yellow stars, these Jews arrive at a Nazi concentration camp in 1944.

A SPECIAL GIFT

Throughout 1941 and the first half of 1942, Otto and Edith Frank tried to keep their daughters' lives as normal as possible. When Jews were forbidden to attend school with Christian children, for example, they sent Margot and Anne to a Jewish school. They also encouraged the girls to play with their friends and enjoy themselves.

Anne turned thirteen in June of 1942. On her birthday, family, friends, and schoolmates showered her with gifts and attention. Of all the presents, one of her favorites was an autograph book with a pretty, red-checked cover. But Anne did not want to use the little book to collect autographs. Instead, she chose to use it as a very personal, very private diary.

Anne (second from right) with her teacher and classmates in 1940

In one of her earliest diary entries, Anne noted, "Writing in a diary is a really strange experience for someone like me. Not only because I've never written anything before, but also because it seems to me that later on neither I nor anyone else will be interested in the musing of a thirteen-year-old schoolgirl. Oh well, it doesn't matter. I feel like writing, and I have an even greater need to get all kinds of things off my chest."

Dear Diary

On June 12, 1942, Anne made her first diary entry (addressed to the diary): "I hope I will be able to confide everything to you, as I have never been able to confide in anyone, and I hope you will be a great source of comfort and support."

Anne Frank's diary

Anne Frank in May 1942, just two months before she and her family went into hiding

Anne wrote in her diary as if she were writing to a very close friend, someone she trusted completely. "Dearest Kitty," she once wrote, "I'm such an idiot. I forgot that I haven't yet told you the story of my one true love." Another entry begins: "My dearest Kitty, At long, long last, I can sit quietly at my table before the crack in the window frame and write you everything, everything I want to say." In page after page, she created a record of her activities and her innermost thoughts and feelings. When she was not writing in the diary, she kept it locked. Years later, her friend Lies Goslar admitted, "I was always very curious to know what was in the diary, but she never showed it to anyone."

THE FAMILY IS THREATENED

Although Anne's parents threw birthday parties and provided other trappings of a normal life, they could not pretend that Jews were safe in Amsterdam. One night, Anne and Hello Silberberg, her latest boyfriend, went for a walk and did not return until 8:10, ten minutes after the curfew for Jews. Otto and Edith were frantic. According to Anne, her cheerful, easygoing father "was furious. He said it was very wrong of me not to get home on time. I had to promise to be home by ten to eight in the future."

The Franks' problems became much worse on July 5, 1942. That day, they received a letter ordering sixteen-year-old Margot to report to a Nazi "labor camp" immediately. Otto and Edith were stunned. Allowing Margot to be **deported** was unthinkable, but how could they prevent the Germans from tearing the family apart? The Franks could not run away because

Hitler's "Final Solution"

In 1942, the Nazis decided that harassing Jews and killing them in small numbers was not enough. If they were going to rid the world of Jews, they had to be more efficient. Led by Reinhard Heydrich, the Nazis developed what they called the "Final Solution." In Germany and other parts of Europe, they built extermination camps—huge killing factories where staggering numbers of people could be slaughtered all at once. When the camps were completed, the Nazis began killing people—mostly Jews—by the millions.

In 1943, Jewish women and children arrive at Auschwitz, a Nazi concentration camp in Poland. Many were killed immediately.

Jews were forbidden to leave the country. Yet if they ignored Margot's deportation order, she would be taken away by force. They could see only one solution— go into hiding.

Without Anne or Margot's knowledge, Otto and Edith had already prepared for this possibility. Months earlier, Otto found a hiding place—the unoccupied attic of the building that housed his business. Slowly and carefully (so as not to attract the attention of the Nazis), he took furniture, food, and other essentials to the hideout. By the time Margot received her summons, the family was ready to "disappear."

CHAPTER 5

THE SECRET ANNEX

The Franks left their apartment for the last time on Monday, July 6, 1942. Writing in her diary two days later, Anne recalled, "A warm rain fell throughout the day. The four of us were wrapped in so many layers of clothes it looked as if we were going off to spend the night in a refrigerator, and all that just so we could take more clothes with us. No Jew in our situation would dare leave the house with a suitcase full of clothes. . . . I was suffocating even before we left the house, but no one bothered to ask me how I felt."

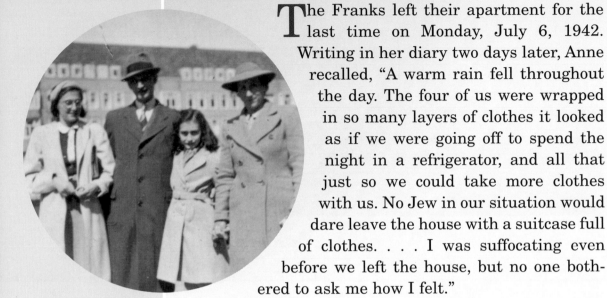

The Frank family in 1941

BECOMING FUGITIVES

For over two years, the Franks and four friends lived in the attic of 263 Prinsengracht (center).

Margot left first. She took off her star and rode her bicycle (an illegal and highly dangerous activity for a Jew) to the hiding place and arrived before the others. Otto, Edith, and Anne walked. Hoping to pass as shoppers, each person carried a few possessions in shopping bags. Anne also carried a schoolbag that held her diary and a few other important items.

As the three walked, Otto and Edith told Anne where they were headed. They also explained that four of Otto's most trusted employees—Johannes Kleiman, Miep Gies, Bep Voskuijl, and Victor Kugler—were expecting them. Mr. Frank had already talked to these employees, and they had agreed to do whatever

they could to help their Jewish friends.

When the Franks arrived at Opekta, Mrs. Gies led them upstairs to their new home. According to Anne, the five attic rooms were "so full of stuff I can't find the words to describe it. All the cardboard boxes that had been sent to the office in the last few months were piled on the floors and beds. . . . If we wanted to sleep in properly made beds that night, we had to get going and straighten up the mess."

Margot and Edith were overwhelmed by the events of the morning. They collapsed onto bare mattresses while Anne and Otto took care of the two highest priorities—unpacking and sewing makeshift curtains from scraps of cloth so no one could see into their hideout.

Mr. Frank Asks for Help

Otto Frank knew that when his family went into hiding, they would need help from people on the outside—people who could discreetly bring them food and other essentials, people who could be trusted to keep a secret.

Miep Gies remembered the day Otto asked for her help. As she recalled: "He [Otto] took a breath and asked, 'Miep, are you willing to take on the responsibility of taking care of us while we are in hiding?'

'Of course,' I answered.

"There is a look between two people once or twice in a lifetime that cannot be described by words. That look passed between us. 'Miep, for those who help Jews, the punishment is harsh; imprisonment, perhaps—'

"I cut him off. I said, 'of course.' I meant it. . . .

"I asked no further questions. The less I knew, the less I could say in an interrogation. . . . I felt no curiosity. I had given my word."

The room where Anne Frank slept while in hiding

SETTLING IN

At first, life in the "secret annex"—Anne's name for the attic—seemed like an adventure to the thirteen-year-old girl. Even so, she was constantly afraid that the Nazis

Auguste Van Pels

Hermann Van Pels

Peter Van Pels

would find and punish them, maybe even kill them. And she knew that there was no going back to their old life. The Franks would stay in hiding until the war ended—or they were discovered.

A week after the Franks became fugitives, three of their Jewish friends—Hermann and Auguste Van Pels and their teenaged son, Peter—joined them in the secret annex. Five months later, a Jewish dentist named Fritz Pfeffer moved in as well. By November, the tiny attic sheltered eight very frightened and anxious Jews.

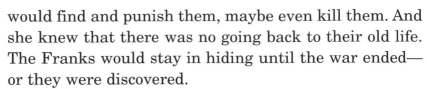

Names in the Diary

Anne realized that her diary, if found, might incriminate the Jews who were hiding with her. To disguise their identities, she used fictitious names for some of the people in the secret annex. Hermann, Auguste, and Peter Van Pels became Putti, Petronella, and Peter van Daan. Fritz Pfeffer became Albert Dussel. Anne also made up names for the non-Jewish people who were helping the Franks and the others survive, and who might also be punished if the diary was found. When her diary was published, Otto Frank chose to include the fictitious names.

Altogether, only a few people knew about the secret annex—the eight people who were hiding there and the "helpers" who brought them food and information. To prevent others from discovering their secret, the group observed many rules: make no noise during the day, when a worker or visitor to the offices might get suspicious; keep the windows covered at all times; do not flush the toilet during working hours; never go outside, for any reason. "Whatever we do," Anne wrote, "we're very afraid the neighbors might hear or see us."

GETTING THROUGH EACH DAY

The fugitives' days were carefully planned to avoid detection. On regular workdays, when employees of Opekta would be in the building, they woke early and took turns in the bathroom, being sure to finish before workers arrived at 8:30. Until lunchtime, they walked on tiptoe, spoke in whispers, and occupied themselves with quiet activities. Anne, Margot, and Peter usually read or did schoolwork (Otto insisted his daughters continue their education), or they helped the adults pare potatoes and clean vegetables for a meal.

At some point in the morning, Miep Gies (who worked downstairs in the office), made an excuse to leave work on an errand. She went out, bought food for the eight fugitives, and hid it under her desk until lunchtime. Then, at 12:30 p.m., when the other

Fritz Pfeffer

Otto Frank (center, seated) in the 1930s with the office workers who would later help him, his family, and his friends hide from the Nazis. Standing, from left, are Johannes Kleiman and Victor Kugler. Seated, from left, are Miep Gies and Bep Voskuijl.

How Much Did Anne Know?

The Germans did not publicize the purpose of their extermination camps, and they certainly did not tell captive Jews that they were being taken there to die. Instead, they usually said the Jews were going to "work camps." This deception has led some people to wonder how much Anne really knew about the extermination camps. Perhaps, some have thought, she was spared the knowledge of what was in store for her.

Unfortunately, there can be no doubt that Anne was well informed. In October 1942, she wrote, "Our many Jewish friends . . . are being taken away in droves. The Gestapo is treating them very roughly and transporting them in cattle cars to [concentration camps]. . . . The people get almost nothing to eat [or] drink, . . . and there's only one toilet and sink for several thousand people. . . . Escape is almost impossible. . . . We assume that most of them are being murdered. The English radio says they're being gassed. Perhaps that's the quickest way to die. . . . I feel terrible."

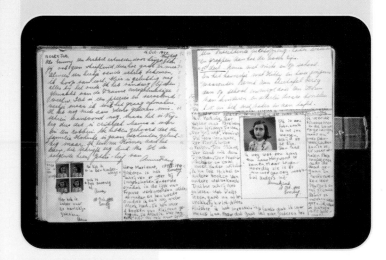

Pages from Anne
Frank's diary, 1942

employees were out of the building for an hour, one or more of the helpers—Miep and Jan Gies, Bep Voskuijl, Johannes Kleiman, and Victor Kugler—went up to the attic. Bringing food, news of the outside world, and library books, the visitors were most welcome. Sometimes they even brought work for their Jewish friends to do—a bit of filing, a little invoicing, anything to keep them busy. Promptly at 1:30 p.m., the visitors returned to work, while those in the secret annex began four more hours of quiet. They were very relieved when the workday ended, and they did not have to worry as much about being discovered.

When the eight people went to bed at night, sleep did not come easily. The **Allies** were bombing military targets in the Netherlands as well as in Germany, and the sounds of planes, bombs, and anti-aircraft fire terrified the group. Every little noise in their building was equally frightening—perhaps someone was coming to arrest or shoot them! After each long night ended, Anne and the others got out of bed exhausted and began another day of hiding.

A Close Call

The Franks and the others in hiding were extremely fearful of burglars. Being robbed, however, was not what frightened them. Instead, they feared that a robbery would lead to the police being involved. Authorities searching the building for burglars might find the fugitives instead.

Criminals did break into the building a few times while the Franks were hiding in the attic. A burglary in April 1944 led to an especially close call. Someone alerted the police, who searched the building thoroughly. When they came to the door leading to the secret annex, an officer rattled the knob and tried to open it. Fortunately, the door was locked, so the police turned away. They had no idea that behind that little gray door, eight Jews were trembling with fright.

During these difficult, frightening times, Anne's diary provided an outlet for some of her anxiety. Nearly every week—sometimes every day—she spent hours writing in it. Sometimes she described her daily life in detail or recorded funny or annoying conversations that had taken place in the annex. Other times, she poured out her feelings about her family and her companions, the terrible changes taking place in her world, and her struggle to live up to her own expectations and those of others. "So far you truly have been a great source of comfort to me," she wrote on September 28, 1942. ". . . now I can hardly wait for those moments when I'm able to write in you. . . . Oh, I'm so glad I brought you along!"

CHAPTER 6

ARREST

The Frank family and their friends lived in the secret annex for twenty-five months—over two years. Anne continued to write in her diary, and she and her companions continued to fear the worst and hope for the best. When Anne turned fifteen in the summer of 1944, she felt old beyond her years and deeply changed by the long, frightening months in hiding. "I have been through things," she wrote, "that hardly anyone has undergone."

Anne's diary entry for Tuesday, August 1, 1944, is an especially thoughtful one. In it, she described herself as having a noisy, lively side that everyone knew and a quieter, more serious side that she revealed only in her diary. She also wrote that she struggled to be a better person but often became angry and annoyed with the people around her. The entry ended with these words: "[I] keep trying to find a way to become what I'd like to be and what I could be if… if only there were no other people in the world."

The stairs to the secret annex were hidden behind this moveable bookcase.

This diary entry is the last one that Anne Frank ever wrote. Just days later—on August 4, 1944—a German policeman and four Dutch Nazis raided the building at 263 Prinsengracht. Brushing quickly past the startled employees, they went directly to the Franks' hiding place, where they ransacked the little rooms and arrested all eight people. The Frank family and the others were herded down the stairs and forced

Who Betrayed Anne Frank?

After the war, the Dutch government arrested and punished people who had delivered Jews to their Nazi tormentors. The government investigated the betrayal of the Franks but never had enough information to make any formal accusations.

Since then, various theories have identified the person who betrayed the Franks and their friends as the warehouse foreman, a neighbor, and the wife of an Opekta employee. A recent theory claims that Tonny Ahlers, a Dutch Nazi who did business with Otto Frank and disliked him intensely, was the culprit. He and other suspects, however, are now dead, so the identity of the betrayer may never be known for sure.

into a windowless police truck. Numb with shock, the prisoners rode to the Nazi police station in silence.

Later that day, when they felt safe enough to go upstairs, Miep Gies, her husband Jan, and Bep Voskuijl crept up to the secret annex. They found a terrible mess—furniture in disarray, clothing strewn about, and cupboards and drawers emptied. Seeing scattered pages of Anne's diary, Mrs. Gies picked them up and took them downstairs. As she put them in her desk drawer, she told Miss Voskuijl, "I'll keep everything safe for Anne until she comes back."

"I Am Not a Hero"

Miep Gies has often been hailed as a hero, but she was never comfortable with this title. "I am not a hero," she wrote. "I stand at the end of the long, long line of good Dutch people who did what I did or more—much more—during those dark and terrible times. . . . I willingly did what I could to help. My husband did as well. It was not enough." Far from feeling like a hero, Mrs. Gies felt a "great and abiding sorrow" over her failure to save her friends' lives.

Mrs. Gies knew her friends were in grave danger and might well be headed for death. Still determined to help, Miep Gies made one last attempt to save them. Risking arrest, imprisonment, perhaps even a bullet in the head, she went to the police station the next day. Once there, she asked for the arresting officer and tried to buy freedom for her friends. The officer was not interested. When he ordered her to leave, Mrs. Gies knew she could do no more.

THE CAMPS

Within a few days, the captive Jews were loaded into a locked train car and shipped to Westerbork, a concentration camp in the northeast region of the Netherlands. Westerbork was a "police transit camp"—a temporary holding place for prisoners on their way to death camps in other countries.

The Westerbork concentration camp

The Franks did not stay there long. On September 3, 1944, they and over one thousand other prisoners were herded into cattle cars and taken on a nightmarish train ride that lasted three nights and two days.

According to a woman who was with the Franks, dozens of people were smashed together. Their cattle car was so crowded that those who tried to sit or lie down were stepped upon. The woman recalled that "many people, among them the Frank girls, slept leaning against their mother or father." She also remembered that the doors on the cars were bolted shut from the outside. The only light came from a candle in a can that hung from the ceiling. There was no food, only a little straw on the floor, and a pail for a toilet. According to this same prisoner, the pail "was filled in the first hour and then spilled over. With seventy people it was a terrible mess, with everything soaking wet. . . . You can imagine how much it stank." Many did not survive the grueling trip. "It was simply a death train," the woman said. "People died [while] underway, and there were many who were dead when we arrived."

The train's final destination was Auschwitz (in Poland), perhaps the most infamous of all extermination camps. A sign over its gate declared, "Work makes you free," a statement intended to lull new arrivals into thinking they had entered a labor camp. The sign, however, was a lie. New arrivals to the camp were entering a killing factory.

One survivor of the Auschwitz camp later described her arrival: "We stumbled out, and I had the feeling I had arrived in

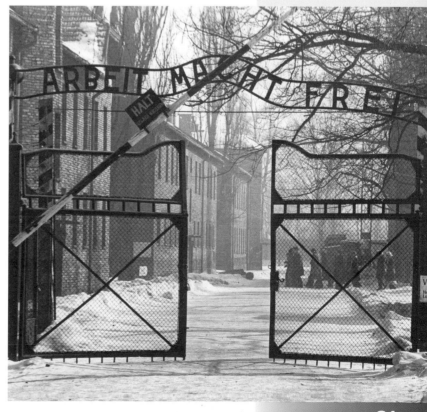

The gates of the Auschwitz concentration camp in Poland. The words above the gate read, *Arbeit Macht Frei*—"Work Makes You Free."

The "Showers"

At Auschwitz, camp guards murdered their victims in a horrific but efficient way. First, they took hundreds (or thousands) of new arrivals into a large courtyard and told the captives to undress so they could take showers. The guards promised the prisoners clean clothes and hot coffee after showering and even gave fake soap to some people to make their lies more believable. The "soap," however, turned out to be stone.

Once the prisoners were naked, they were ordered into a huge chamber. A sign over the door read, "Shower Room." As the prisoners entered, however, many realized it was not a shower room at all—they were going to their deaths. The victims made desperate attempts to escape but were relentlessly herded into the gas chamber by guards wielding whips and clubs. Finally, the guards bolted the doors and released a deadly gas called Zyklon B into the chamber.

According to one witness, "You would hear cries and shouts as the people within began to fight against each other and to beat at the walls. This goes on for two minutes—then complete silence, nothing more." Every man, woman, and child inside was dead.

hell. It was night, chimneys were burning with huge bright flames. The SS [Nazi officers] beat everybody with sticks and guns. . . . Then the selection began." The "selection" determined who would die within the next few hours and who would live, at least for a while. The children, the weak, and the old were in the first group. They were sent to the gas chambers by the hundreds and thousands, their bodies burned in huge furnaces.

Those who were not selected were separated by sex, with males and females being sent to different parts of the camp. Struggling to catch one last glimpse of his family as he was separated from them, Otto finally saw his eldest daughter in the crowd. Years later, he said, "I shall remember the look in Margot's eyes all my life." He never saw her, Edith, or Anne again.

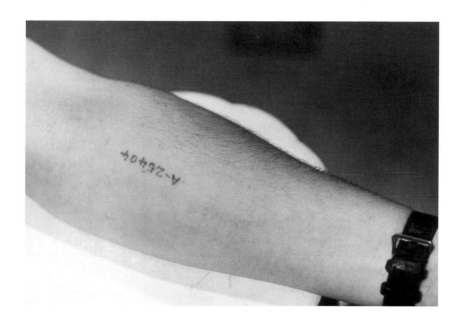

At Auschwitz and other concentration camps, prisoners who were not killed immediately were tattooed with an identification number. Camp survivors carried these tattoos for the rest of their lives.

After being torn away from Otto, the Frank women were "processed," along with hundreds of others. In a series of steps intended to humiliate, hurt, and dehumanize the prisoners, guards first tattooed a number on each woman's arm. Considered "non-persons," the women would now be identified by their numbers, not their names. Next, after making the women strip, the guards shaved them head to foot, cruelly pulling out hair and cutting tender skin. The guards then herded the cowering prisoners into showers. (In this case, the showers sprayed water, but later "showers" would be gas chambers.) After the showers, the women were forced to jump into a tank of disinfectant. Finally, they were herded past huge piles of clothing. Each woman was handed a few items—perhaps just underpants and a shirt, maybe a skirt or a dress—to cover her nakedness.

The Fires

At Auschwitz, thousands of people were gassed every day. To dispose of the bodies, the Nazis used almost fifty crematoria—large ovens that could each hold about three bodies and could reduce the bodies to ashes in half an hour. The ovens had to run nearly twenty-four hours a day to keep up with all the bodies.

Sometimes there were simply too many bodies for the ovens to handle. In such cases, the Nazis forced their prisoners to dig huge pits in the ground. Then they threw in corpses by the thousands, added oil or alcohol, and torched the gruesome tangle of human flesh. So many bodies were burned in each pit that channels had to be dug to drain off the fat. If the fires were burning too slowly, the fire-tenders poured the human fat back on the pile to make the flames burn hotter and faster. The sight and smell of these ghastly fires haunted many survivors for the rest of their lives.

Crematoria at a German concentration camp

After being processed, the trembling women were sent to the overcrowded, disease-ridden barracks of Birkenau, the part of Auschwitz where women were imprisoned and most of the gassings took place. There, they had little to do but wait—to be gassed, to die of starvation or disease, to be sent to another camp. A survivor recalled that time: "You saw, all the time, the furnace with a huge flame. You smelled the scorched flesh. And everywhere you saw the despair. It was a terrible, hopeless existence."

Neither Anne nor Margot was gassed at Birkenau. Instead, after almost two months, they were taken from their mother, loaded onto another cattle car, and sent to Bergen-Belsen, a concentration camp in Germany.

This 1945 photograph shows survivors of a Nazi concentration camp in Austria that has been liberated by Allied forces.

Living conditions at the German camp were even worse than at Birkenau. When the girls arrived, they were herded into a large tent with dozens of other women. The tent was pitched on wet clay and had no light, heat, beds, running water, or toilets. One night, a violent storm blew the tent down, forcing

Margot, Anne, and the others to keep warm by huddling beneath the collapsed canvas for several days. They were eventually moved to a sturdier structure, but conditions were still terrible. Infectious diseases—**typhus**, scarlet fever, pneumonia, and dysentery—were rampant. With no medical care or disease control available, thousands died.

THE STRUGGLE ENDS

In February 1945, Anne's old friend Hanneli Goslar learned that she and Anne were in different parts of the same camp, separated by a few strands of barbed wire. Hanneli managed to get a message to Anne, and they met by the fence. Hanneli later remembered that "it wasn't the same Anne. She was a broken girl. . . . It was so terrible. She immediately began to cry, and [believing that her parents were dead] she told me, 'I don't have any parents anymore.'" During that meeting, Anne also told her friend, "'We don't have anything at all to eat here, . . . and we are cold; we don't have any clothes and I've gotten very thin and they shaved my hair.'"

By that time, Anne was critically ill with typhus. According to another survivor, Anne had cast off her lice-infested clothes in her delirious state. A single, thin blanket was her only protection from the winter cold.

Not long after Anne's meeting with Hanneli, in March 1945, the Frank girls died—first Margot and then Anne. The exact details of

These prisoners at the Bergen-Belsen concentration camp are removing clothes from dead victims to burn as fuel.

their deaths are not known. People were nearby at the time, but many of them died, too. Most of those who survived—all of whom watched hundreds or thousands perish at Bergen-Belsen—did not remember specific details about these two deaths. One fellow inmate had only this recollection: "First, Margot had fallen out of bed onto the stone floor. She couldn't get up anymore. Anne died a day later."

One of the women in the barracks with Anne and Margot could not remember exactly when the girls died. "Dying," she explained, "was the order of the day in Bergen-Belsen." She was sure, however, about what happened after they died: "The dead were always carried outside, laid down in front of the barracks, and when you were let out in the morning to go to the latrine, you had to walk past them. . . . Possibly it was on one of those trips to the latrine that I walked past the bodies of the Frank sisters, one or both—I don't know. At the time, I assumed that the bodies of the Frank girls had also been put down in front of the barracks. . . . A huge hole would be dug and they were thrown into it. That I'm sure of. That must have been their fate, because that's what happened with other people."

This photograph of a mass grave at Bergen-Belson was taken in April 1945, just a few weeks after Anne Frank died.

CHAPTER 7

AFTER THE WAR

In late January of 1945, Otto Frank and dozens of other inmates were lined up in front of a firing squad at Auschwitz. Just as an officer was about to give the order to shoot, a series of explosions could be heard beyond the camp gate. Members of the Allied forces had arrived. The Nazis forgot about their prisoners and ran for their lives. Just seconds away from being executed, Otto Frank instead became a Holocaust survivor.

The war in Europe ended in May of that year, and Otto found his way back to Amsterdam. While heading home, he learned that Edith had died in Auschwitz. He remained hopeful, however, that his two daughters, Margot and Anne, were still alive.

In October 1945, Otto received a letter from a Bergen-Belsen survivor bringing the worst possible news—Margot and Anne were dead. Miep Gies was with Otto at the Opekta offices when he learned that he was the only living member of his family. According to Mrs. Gies, soon after Mr. Frank received the news, she opened the desk drawer where she had hidden Anne's papers nearly a year earlier. She knew that Anne would never return to claim them. "I took out all the papers, placing the little red-orange checkered diary on top, and carried everything into Mr. Frank's office. . . . I held out the diary and the papers to him. I said, 'Here is your daughter Anne's legacy to you.'"

A prisoner at Bergen-Belsen cannot take another step.

THIS IS THE SITE OF
THE INFAMOUS BELSEN CONCENTRATION CAMP
Liberated by the British on 15 April 1945.

10,000 UNBURIED DEAD WERE FOUND HERE.
ANOTHER 13,000 HAVE SINCE DIED,
ALL OF THEM VICTIMS OF THE
GERMAN NEW ORDER IN EUROPE,
AND AN EXAMPLE OF NAZI KULTUR.

After Allied forces arrived in 1945, the Bergen-Belsen concentration camp was destroyed to prevent typhus from spreading. A sign was erected to remind the world of what happened within the camp.

A DIARY BECOMES A BOOK

Filled with grief, Otto Frank spent many hours with Anne's diary. As he lovingly organized loose papers, he learned for the first time about the private feelings and thoughts his daughter had confided to her diary. He treasured every word—the diary was all that was left of his child. Wanting to keep Anne's memory alive and share her words with others, he copied several entries by hand and sent them to his surviving relatives in Switzerland. Then a friend put the material into typewritten form, which Otto sent to friends. People began urging him to publish Anne's diary.

From reading his daughter's own words, Otto knew her wish was to have her thoughts reach out to others: "After the war I'd like to publish a book called The Secret Annex. It remains to be seen whether I'll succeed, but my diary can serve as the basis." Despite these words, Otto hesitated, partly because Anne had always kept her diary private, and partly because many of her entries were very personal and some were critical of her family and friends. Eventually, however, Mr. Frank decided that Anne would want her work to be published.

Finding a publisher was not easy—the war was over and most publishers thought readers did not want to be reminded of that awful time. In 1946, however, a historian named Jan Romein read the diary. He was so touched by Anne's words that he wrote about them in a newspaper article. That article—"A Child's Voice"—caught the attention of a Dutch publisher.

In 1947, Anne Frank's diary was published in the Netherlands. The book achieved great popularity among the Dutch, who had also been victimized by the Nazis. Over the next several years, the diary was published in many languages. An English translation was published with the title *Anne Frank: The Diary of a Young Girl*. Anne's words can now be read in at least fifty-five languages, and her diary has become one of the best-selling books of all time.

In 1955, two American playwrights, Frances Goodrich and Albert Hackett, wrote a play entitled *The Diary of Anne Frank* that was based on the diary. The play had such a powerful and important message that it won the Pulitzer Prize for Drama in 1956. Even now—a half-century later—the play continues to move audiences wherever it is performed. A movie with the same title, also based on the diary, was released in 1959.

GENOCIDE THEN AND NOW

Almost six million European Jews lost their lives in the **genocide** known as the Holocaust. Millions of other Europeans, including Gypsies, Poles, and Russians, were also exterminated. Some were killed because of their ethnic ancestry, others because of their political beliefs. Hundreds of thousands more, including homosexuals and disabled children and adults, were put to death as well. Like the Jews, they were all considered by the Nazis to be "non-persons," "bloodsuckers," and "objects of disgust"—vermin that the world would be better off without.

The Holocaust's Death Toll

The Holocaust decimated centuries of Jewish life and culture by wiping out 60 percent of Europe's Jewish population. The figures below indicate the Holocaust's death toll in individual countries.

Country (Defined by prewar borders)	Jewish population, September 1939	Number of Jews dead by 1945	Percentage of Jews dead
Poland	3,300,000	2,500,000	85.0
Soviet Union (Occupied Area)	2,100,000	1,500,000	71.4
Romania	850,000	425,000	50.0
Hungary	404,000	200,000	49.5
Czechoslovakia	315,000	260,000	82.5
France*	300,000	90,000	30.0
Germany	210,000	170,000	81.0
Lithuania	150,000	135,000	90.0
The Netherlands*	150,000	103,000	68.7
Latvia	95,000	85,000	89.5
Belgium*	90,000	40,000	44.4
Greece	75,000	60,000	80.0
Yugoslavia	75,000	55,000	73.3
Austria	60,000	40,000	66.6
Italy*	57,000	15,000	26.3
Bulgaria	50,000	7,000	14.0
Miscellaneous**	20,000	6,000	30.0
Totals	8,301,000	5,991,000	72.2

*Figures include Jewish refugees
**Denmark, Estonia, Luxembourg, Norway, and the city of Danzig, Poland
(Adapted from *The Burden Of Guilt: A Short History of Germany, 1914-1945*, by Hannah Vogt, published by Oxford University Press, 1964; and *L'zecher*, published by Sdu Uitgeverij Koninginnegracht, 1995.)

In the years between 1933 and 1945, the Nazis ruthlessly and systematically harassed, imprisoned, tortured, and killed millions of human beings. They enslaved their victims, subjected them to inhumane medical experiments, forced them to witness the executions of their loved ones, and ultimately slaughtered them. These savage crimes were not caused by anything the victims did. Instead, they were the result of prejudices toward people who were considered "different" from others. By exploiting the power of these prejudices, the Nazis made scapegoats of the innocent and the weak as they fanned the flames of "Aryan supremacy" and German nationalism.

The Nazis, however, were neither the first nor the last group of people to commit genocide. As long as people have felt entitled to destroy fellow human beings on the basis of real or imagined differences, genocide has been with us. Young as she was, Anne Frank recognized this sad fact of the human condition. On May 3, 1944—three

Genocide Today

Genocide continues to plague our world. In the last decade alone, heinous crimes against humanity have caused a million deaths. In 1994, in a fury of ethnic and political hatred, the Hutus exterminated about 800,000 Tutsis in the African country of Rwanda. From 1999 to 2001, in Eastern Europe, Yugoslavian Serbs in the region of Kosovo murdered thousands of ethnic Albanians as part of an "ethnic cleansing" campaign intended to rid Yugoslavia of Muslims and other non-Serbian groups. Halfway around the world, meanwhile, Indonesian soldiers were killing thousands of Timorese in the Indonesian region of East Timor.

A house in Indonesia burns in 2001 as one group of people tries to eliminate another.

months before she was taken away to Auschwitz—Anne wrote, "There's a destructive urge in people, the urge to rage, murder, and kill. And until all of humanity. . . undergoes a [great change], wars will continue to be waged, and everything that has been carefully built up . . . will be cut down and destroyed, only to start all over again!"

Despite such a sobering statement—one that the horrors of World War II certainly seemed to prove accurate—Anne also believed that people had the capacity for making meaningful, positive changes. "How wonderful it is," she wrote, "that no one has to wait, but can start right now to gradually change the world!"

Over half a century has passed since Anne Frank wrote these optimistic words, and time has not lessened their power. In 1999, as United Nations (UN) secretary general Kofi Annan signed the Anne Frank Peace Declaration, he paid tribute to her message: "Anne Frank's eternal words have inspired people of all ages, religions and nationalities, but they resound most powerfully among the young. . . . If Anne Frank, in her living hell, could summon the will to imagine a better, peaceful world, a future free of suffering and persecution, then surely we can summon the will to make that day come to pass."

A statue of Anne Frank now stands in the Dutch city of Amsterdam.

TIMELINE

1921	Adolf Hitler becomes the leader of the Nazi Party in Germany
1929	Great Depression begins; Annelies (Anne) Marie Frank is born on June 12 in Frankfurt, Germany
1933	Adolf Hitler becomes chancellor of Germany; the Franks move to the Netherlands to escape Nazi persecution of German Jews
1940	German troops invade and conquer the Netherlands in five days
1941	Nazi authorities begin widespread persecution of Dutch Jews
1942	Anne receives a diary for her thirteenth birthday; on July 5, Margot Frank is ordered to report to a labor camp; on July 6, the entire Frank family goes into hiding
1944	On August 4, Nazis raid the Franks' hiding place; the Frank family is sent to the Auschwitz concentration camp in Poland; Anne and Margo Frank are eventually sent to the Bergen-Belsen concentration camp in Germany
1945	In January, Edith Frank dies at Auschwitz; three weeks later, Otto Frank is freed from the camp by Allied troops; in March, Margo and Anne Frank die of typhus at Bergen-Belsen; on April 15, Allied troops liberate Bergen-Belsen
1946	Historian Jan Romein praises Anne's diary in a newspaper article
1947	Anne Frank's diary is first published, in Dutch, with the title *Het Achterhuis* ("The House Behind")
1952	The first U.S. edition of Anne's diary is published, with the title *Anne Frank: Diary of a Young Girl*
1955	A play adaptation of Anne's diary, *The Diary of Anne Frank*, premieres in New York City
1956	*The Diary of Anne Frank* is awarded the Pulitzer Prize for drama
1963	Otto Frank and his second wife establish Anne Frank Fonds, a charitable organization in Switzerland
1980	Otto Frank dies on August 19

GLOSSARY

Allies: the countries, including the United States, Great Britain, and the Soviet Union, that fought against Germany, Japan, and Italy during World War II.

anti-Semitism: hostility toward Jews.

concentration camps: places where people such as prisoners of war, political prisoners, or persecuted minorities are held, often under harsh conditions.

deported: forced to leave the country.

dictator: a leader who exerts absolute control over a country's government and the lives of its citizens.

genocide: the deliberate destruction of an ethnic, racial, cultural, or political group.

Great Depression: a severe economic slump during the 1930s, when large numbers of people in many countries lost their jobs and savings.

Hanukkah: a Jewish religious festival that usually takes place in December.

Holocaust: the massive killing of Jews by the Nazis before and during World War II.

inflation: the rise of prices for goods.

Nazis: members of the National Socialist German Workers Party, a political party founded in Germany in 1919 and led by Adolf Hitler from 1921 to 1945.

parliament: a legislative body made up of elected representatives.

persecute: to harass or harm a person, often because of the person's race, religion, gender, sexual orientation, or political beliefs.

pogroms: organized massacres of Jews, which occurred first in Russia in the 1880s and occurred there again in the early twentieth century.

prejudiced: having opinions (which are usually negative) that are based on preconceived ideas rather than facts.

propaganda: ideas or information used to help or hurt a particular cause.

refugees: people who flee a place because of war, persecution, or other dangers in order to find a safe place to live.

synagogue: a place where Jews worship.

typhus: an infectious disease caused by germs that are carried by fleas and lice.

TO FIND OUT MORE

BOOKS

Altman, Linda Jacobs. *The Holocaust in History (series)*. New Jersey: Enslow Publishers, 2003.

Bachrach, Susan D. *Tell Them We Remember: The Story of the Holocaust.* Boston: Little, Brown & Company, 1994.

Frank, Anne. *Anne Frank: The Diary of a Young Girl.* New York: Doubleday, 1995.

Frank, Anne. *Anne Frank's Tales from the Secret Annex.* New York: Bantam Books, 2003.

Gottfried, Ted. *Children of the Slaughter: Young People of the Holocaust.* Brookfield, CT.: Twenty-First Century Books, 2001.

Hondius, Dienke. *Anne Frank in the World, 1929–1945.* New York: Alfred A. Knopf, 2001.

Rogasky, Barbara. *Smoke and Ashes: The Story of the Holocaust.* New York: Holiday House, 2002.

van der Rol, Ruud and Verhoeven, Rian. *Anne Frank: Beyond the Diary.* New York: Puffin Books, 1999.

Wukovits, John F. *World War II in Europe (World History).* San Diego: Lucent Books, 2004.

INTERNET SITES

Anne Frank Center USA
www.annefrank.com
Offers historical background and biographical information on the Frank family.

The Anne Frank Internet Guide
come.to/annefrank
For internet resources on Anne Frank.

Jewish Virtual Library: Hitler and the Jewish Question
www.us-israel.org/jsource/Holocaust/hitjew.html
Includes an excerpt of a speech about Jews given by Adolf Hitler on January 30, 1939.

Museum of Tolerance's Online Multimedia Learning Center: Frequently Asked Questions
motlc.wiesenthal.com/resources/questions/index.html#2
Provides information about the Holocaust, including a timeline, glossary, and answers to commonly asked questions.

United States Holocaust Memorial Museum: Learning About the Holocaust
www.ushmm.org/education/forstudents/
For information on anti-Semitism, Adolf Hitler's rise to power, and the Holocaust and its aftermath.

INDEX (continued)

About the Author

Jonatha A. Brown has a broad background in writing and editing, much of it as a freelancer helping corporations develop interactive computer-based training programs. A native of Rochester, New York, Jonny holds a BA in English from St. Lawrence University in Canton, New York. She currently lives in Phoenix, Arizona, with her husband and two dogs. She is delighted to be taking a break from corporate life by working with horses and writing books for children.